PHANTOM
GANG

About the Author

Ciarán O'Rourke was born in 1991 and took a degree in English and History at Trinity College, Dublin. He received a Masters in English and American Studies from Oxford in 2014, as well as a doctorate on William Carlos Williams at his alma mater in Dublin in 2019. His first collection, *The Buried Breath*, was published by The Irish Pages Press in 2018 and highly commended by the Forward Foundation for Poetry the following year. He currently lives in Galway.

On "Death of a Refugee" in *The Buried Breath*:

"Shocking, visceral, rhythmic, righteous, unforgettable – dark music our age needs to hear."

Dave Lordan, *poet*

PHANTOM GANG

CIARÁN O'ROURKE

THE IRISH PAGES PRESS
2022

Phantom Gang
is first published in hardback
on 15 July 2022.

The Irish Pages Press
129 Ormeau Road
Belfast BT7 1SH
Ireland

www.irishpages.org

Typeset in 14/18 pt Monotype Perpetua
Designed and composed by RV, Belfast. Printed by Bell & Bain, Glasgow.

A CIP catalogue record for this book
is available from The British Library.

Dust-jacket photographs:
Enri Canaj and Ciarán O'Rourke.

ISBN: 978-1-8382018-4-5

Also by Ciarán O'Rourke

The Buried Breath
(2018)

CONTENTS

ROS INBHIR

Let the sky-thin seasons stake their claim

in the ditch of my eyes,
in the flood of my bones,
in the torn out root of my mouth —

I'll move
like light in the dirt, or a lifting lark,
like rain at the edge of your meadowed mind.

CLUAIN CHLÁIR

Imagine winter
like a worm a-slink
in the undercutting ruts

that designate the field.
Imagine
being part of winter there,

the pain behind your eyes
a metonym made flesh
for every sky-sustaining

flex of wind
the thinning ground supplied,
your skin another word

for fog the peaty ice exhaled.
My mind maps out
his death this way, in visionary seasons

turning home – in which
insensate elements
lock the earth,

yet still might learn
to take the shape
of verb and cyclorama,

quickening as sleet:
the thirst and thaw
of sunken roots

his nearest resurrection.
Some creaturely
intelligence, no doubt,

invents these myths
I fabricate as prayer,
but look –

a songthrush answers
emptied air,
spattering the sod.

COILLTE CLOCHAIR

Nothing: the bed his voice
and body both lie down to fill,

the less-than-breath
that's rushing still

to clinch
the fervid hush

that clung to him
for days,

if not, in quiet ways,
for years.

The death bed
summons and depletes

all prior consolations,
like the breeze

that's more a totem here,
which once took lake light

swooping
to the height of heaven,

the turf-stoop stacked to drain
above the field,

and he himself nearby,
at home and all astir

with what the sifting seasons
bring to Leitrim hills,

a rhythm loosening
the earth for work,

a rained-on world
susceptible to life

and even joy, despite
the hazards —

the springtime's
slow release in him

that startles now
by absence, branching

through the room ...
as if Edward Thomas, say,

had wandered with intent
from some mud-

lit, endless
corridor of trees

into a sudden space of clearing,
where the new moon

and every star
are brightened places near at hand,

or into the open echo-
chamber of poetry, perhaps,

where now I find myself,
muttering as though in sleep:

It hurts my skin but captivates
my mind, this haze

of April weather — and no singing
bird to set the darkness free.

CIONN LOCHA

To pick an image intimate
with all of that,

but unconstrained, a picture
blown by recollection

into speaking life,
I gravitate

to the wren's nest:
the swivelled-into,

imbricated gift of it
he found and held,

and how I stared,
infantilised, as though

its convoluting limb of leaves
might disentwine

before my eyes,
or as if

his supple, sappy grip of it,
his own hands

like breathing leaves,
might take to flight

as he raised, after,
its living relic back

to where the breeze rocked
branches sky to sky –

to have the branch-tips
dip again, and lighten

with the inessential system
of the wren's nest

and the memory of wrens.

AN TULACHÁN

Before, I took the corncrake's
half-imagined, famished noise

by some cliff-edge
of Leitrim's dwindling coast

to symbolise
the pleas for breath

his body proffered
angrily

in fits of stillness
near the end,

or else
to lineate

the loss inferred
(if not undone)

by this, the art
of second sighting:

belated revelation
rasping into song,

a frailty remembered
I still depended on.

But now
the corncrake's vanished, too,

its sky-fulfilling,
raking air

no more some dim precarity,
tenaciously beheld,

but poisoned absence
striking deep –

a trace persisting,
permutating, seeping

through the grid.
At night I wake to it,

ubiquitous and close:
time's carcass rising slowly,

speechless in my throat.

ACHADH BHUACHAILL

The land here
dreams in silhouettes

our bodies
learn to read:

as when, in sleet-
grey summer once,

the whole half-hill's
herd of tactful men

stood in
stiff formation,

scuffing the mud
in murmurs,

till the cart for Sligo
swung the gap

and rose to rest
on the sluiced yard-grass

in readiness —
a ticking signal

that set them turning, then,
to work, pinning down

the thin man's
addled legs,

and tautening a disc
of unfrayed rope

to still the violent
fits and cries,

a clench of rip-cloth
passed along

to stem
the babbling mouth

of Michael Maguire,
packed up now

for the madhouse ward,
but long observed,

who for years before
had never heard

the storming alder grove
in spring

or the cuckoo's weather-
piercing word

without a week
of shadow-pacing after,

and whose fingers
always tremored

(the watching boy
remembered later)

like worn metal
in a saucer

or the wings of fleeting poplars,
broken by the rain.

BÉALOIDEAS

The sean-nós songman
hooks a thumb

in each belt-strap, and leans
his hip to the wall

to wait, like a ship
in shallow sands,

so whatever waver,
tilt, or rooting down

the brick-lined room
allows

is his, or comes to rest
with him

as the crowded air
rebuilds to hush,

and soon the song
descends, oh,

with a voice as dark
as the river mouth,

as supple
as winds are deep,

as bitter as hale
on a bed of stones,

as fogged and low
with grief,

like the girl
who buried her shadow,

or the woman who flew
in her sleep,

or the man who's less
than a whisper now,

who once regaled
the seas,

whose lover
was sent to another

for the price of
a penful of sheep.

LATIN

I sent a sheaf of Latin light,
re-built
in frantic likenesses of you,

the whole effect intended
to un-web as need
that knot of quietness

I called my heart:
by nimble
literation of the lines.

The men you sidled close to,
and the nook
from which my winded mind

observed such ease
(the dark I learned to replicate
and wreak)

took flight as sudden sparrow song,
as if to make
of every madding interval

a touch we both could share.
Alone, I pressed
a blinking stone inside my fist,

and willed
your woken glance,
a world away, to raid

some half-forgotten vacancy
for sign of me again,
my residue

a breath,
a far off wave,
collapsing out of sight.

We met above the break,
in foreign night,
and cut

a twisted pictogram,
our limbs
one fractal globe of glass

where suns
that sank forever
in the future tense

now rise to burn
time's writing alphabet
to dust in memory,

a scar on skin.
I comprehend
the elegist too late –

love's ocean
breakers filled
a clodden grave,

and the bird
that sang of yearning
died of hate.

SAPPHO'S MOUTH

Perhaps I'll press
the whole, em-
bittered fruit of it

to Sappho's perfect
mouth, who said
aloud one morning

as the sun lay down
in whispered mists,
something like:

far wingbeats
brought you close,
my heart, delicate

though they were,
and dark the ground
beneath, as the levelled air

grew thin, and
sparrows hummed
in the blood even,

for you came
quick as
a sparrow for me.

THE UNWOMANLY FACE OF WAR

First love, first touch,
first flame fatale,

I only half-remember you
as all my world:

the kite in your voice
I followed,

the ocean
salt I kissed.

Your year-by-year
recourse to reticence

enraged my fitful
poet's pen

to jealous eloquence,
and flights:

I wrote to you
in Latin, or not at all.

Now, your silence
falls in pools about my nights;

my mind peers out
beyond its storming ledge

to find your stone-blue look
of hurt retained

returned again,
as snow-drifts packed the earth

above your mother's grave
and I took my bullish leave.

Later, in shock
and partly manic dream,

I glimpsed, with
some extravagance,

the both of us
(the winter's pain I stung you with)

in the nurse, nineteen,
who smelt the mud

of Stalingrad congeal
in piss-replenished roads of blood

outside her station-door,
and decades after

lived to read
the Crimean sea's calligraphy of blue

in rising lines that slit her square-cut
window-pane in two

for smoke and other signs of war
resumed. *Some days I sit*

and watch, she said,
and wait for waves —

I still don't have a woman's face,
the war took all my years.

Oh but, sleeper, swimmer,
second self,

did you forgive your nightmare lover
his cruelty and tears?

BIRTHDAY

A thousand flocks fly overhead
and all the spring applauds,

our birthday filled with planetary
promise once again —

as Anna Akhmatova writes
of softened frost, the muck of grief

grown wet with dew, and week
by week the blood-blue flowers

bursting into life, wallpaper pictures
howling for the times:

these the gifts you choose
to send instead of news,

sequestered pain
made breathable by light itself:

the light of iron Russia
melting into air...

but a hundred years away
your *all my love*'s the only ghost

I look to find in every poem,
its dance of wings

a cipher, strung
through Anna's riven skies, who sang:

Though the years are drifting rivers,
why do you never change, my love, clear-

skinned and soft on the brimming shore,
your voice as near as day?

Only your eyes are altered now,
stung by the mist of last year's snow.

HISTORY

Our one sick world spins on —
returningly, and slow —

easing gathered greenness
into leaf. Tonight

through tangled heat the swallows weave,
high up and fast, and out of sight.

My undistracted finger strokes
a desk-lit, wooden globe

and hears the running axis
hum beneath.

This dream-beginning
dark is all I know.

Its hand shuts round my heart,
like ice begun to thaw and flow.

Soon the only room's
a river, in which

my swilling mind
reluctantly

resists re-writing you
an apoplectic postcard from the past,

packed in to burst
with half-accusing calotypes

of how and when I loved you most.
Young ghost

at sea, adrift, a human
spangle webbed by wind,

eyes ahead, my blue breath
climbed the swelling tide to find you:

dropped
by a daylight-furling,

freak first wave,
its fist of salt, on the sand:

stunned by the sun
in your swim-suit, laughing.

Your quick, ungainly
beauty stops me even still.

It goes like this, all remiscence.
Made lean, remiss and rancorous

by rage (that brutal, self-forgiving war),
my every season somehow lifts

to breathe, O love, our histories
from off the brimming air.

PORTRAIT IN RED AND BLACK

Weather breaks; and with it, word

of how the terror-states
are savaging the world again

for oil and water – gods
of universal domination.

The near and distant
pandemonia collide

in pallid light that's like
an atmosphere outside our door,

to soak the wind
and tremble every leaf –

till nothing's left
of clarity, but grief

at what the demon wreaked,
and the dreaming beat of rain.

Only the goldfinch
feels alive –

a skeet of colour,
stout as a cloud,

his knuckle and plunge
of plumage stark

against the slipping boughs.
I watch him thrum

and pluck terrifically,
marshalling the morning

with my heart in his mouth.

THE TREE

A poem, which
as the bullets whinnied

through the night
and across the dreaming century

flittered from the cracks
of Fadwa Tuqan's singing heart,

and danced the wind,
and shook the years, eventually

to grapple here, unbesieged
but altered, an ever-changing sigh.

And so: *the tree* (she writes)
regains the blasted field at last,

like a shadow-torch
the ground ignit, that greens

the gravelled air in sun,
and celebrates the rain.

After the bone-dark
hurricane retreats, it lifts

a feast of light, this tree;
and after the ringing walls

break down, its leaves transmit
their murmurs, sounding

like the sea, to say:
the birds, if not the dead, return,

and with birds
the rising days begin,

the rage and ache
we call the spring,

a word for what
the carnage reckoned —

and still the birds returning.

RISE

From Nazareth: *this light*
            in my eyes,
this flame in my blood,
and all the pain
            of Palestine

I speak and gladly give –
            I, the orphan
starving, who heard
the guns invade, the boots
            ring out,

the prison walls resound.
            For at my back
my people sing, like a dove
raised high on woken winds,
            or this flag

of love and history
            our voices carry,
which soon will shake
the mountains, like
            the olive tree in leaf.

A RESISTANCE WRITER
REFLECTS ON HIS LIFE

Variations on poems by Bertolt Brecht, 1898-1956

In the rippling mirror I catch my face:
well-fed and water-logged, an exile's countenance.

Tomorrow's outcast! That shining place,
where, with the girl who god forgot

and drowned, I'll no doubt vanish also,
strange to the ways of your bleating world.

~

But I was something once
no time ahead could fathom:
          a human soul, seduced by need
to paint the boardroom butchers of the age

in lurid colours, my verses shaped
like sleeting fists, my hunger
          like a storm. I lived in rage
and love in equal measure;

my life knew every texture, had
the beat of living history
          a-thrum in it. And I worked
(in my way) like all the rest. At dawn,

the miners dragged their boots in song
along the cobbles; my coal-
          blue fingers smudged
the page in praise.

                    ~

What, today, you call a river
to me was second nature – gifted,
like the grey boughs donning
wind's weather
in a rush above me years before,

or the pounding clouds
that clapped the forest doors
for days,
till birds emerged
to shake the clearing after,
and the rains she kissed me under
disappeared forever.

The touched
earth – volving lovely
down my body –
this, the haunted mist
I breathed involuntarily,
woke to
year by year.

~

My spirit hummed the brightest
in fits of vision built from sense:

when I saw through spinning water-wheels
the village children growing thin,

or when I tuned my pen
to the famished noise of carolling machines.

And so, my last, light-filled request:
to log, if you will, my voice of ink

among their numberless possessions –
the agitators, legislators, the million-

faced and rebel poor, whose words
were sent to the burning marsh,

whose bones were sunk
in a box of zinc.

~

So we come to the hatred
        of arrogant men:

who, strolling from banquet
        to feast in their suits,

hector the nation with rations;
        who promise a reaping

of luck while they're fat, and let
        the fruit rot beneath sheeting;

who evict brittle children onto
        the streets, and wrap them

in data and numbers; who funnel
        society over a cliff

and proclaim their own
        fitness to govern.

I was moved by a hatred
        of arrogant men.

~

The people I love are bright and harsh.
Their fingers stitch the velvet coats.
Their bodies lift the singing roads.

They shake the wheat. They shape the loaf.
They carve the skyline named in stone
for the emperor and the boss.

And they always bite the famine-dirt
when their ledgers lodge a loss —
but they know far more than this, oh yes ...

As the wave unbolts the ocean
and the slave commands the dawn,
my people's hands have threshed the wind,
            their faces creased the sun.

~

What is food for?
        To clothe the hungry
            dream with heat.

What do dreams become?
        A star a stone a fist a mob, to make
            the richest citizens
                tremble in their beds.

What are poems for?
        To fortify the body,
                to weaponise the mind.

What should we remember?
        Amid the chronicle of cruelties,
                my yearning to be kind.

Who is this?
        Brecht: so mean, so dry,
        so stricken, so strung, I could
                sleep (or march)
                till spring.

BRUNETE

In memory of Gerda Taro, 1910-1937

The bursting bullets flung
by two-chinned Franco's smiling men

to pin the heads of children
squatting in the square,

says Langston Hughes, who loved
the rising river-flow

of freedom (jazz) above the rest,
were usually reserved

for the sun-dark beasts of Africa
alone, so fully

did they shake the nerves
and disembowel the flesh:

murder made to mutilate,
the mark of modern times —

a calculation caught and held
in eye-grey revelation

by your blinking fingers, Gerda,
as on the streaming

patchwork floor of the morgue,
or first on the front

in a singeing wind, you stilled
the curling fist and mouth

of innocence itself: a photograph
to document and damn

this rehearsal-round of Hitler's,
Mussolini's morning game ...

a death-hung tipping-point
you windowed in Brunete,

witnessing the world of now
(today) and then, until

the smoking fires
fell again – to blot

the gaze of your body,
and rip

the flinchless camera
from your hands.

MARTÍN CHAMBI

In far Peru, where
the fish-metallic rivers steam

and ten
thousand children

dig the golden earth
in force, for food,

in freedom's name,
a life-wave's crash

away, Martín,
you found your feet

at just fourteen,
and learnt to see.

Impelled by light,
your daughter said,

you set your studio
in reach

of the Incan heights
and peasant skies

you first took breath
beneath, and let them sing.

A dirt-forgotten people
lived within your lens –

and carried on,
with the sun-

beat women
smiling, hauling hay,

the not-quite-quiet
shining

from the Andean giant's
gentle gaze,

or the barefoot organist,
his long-boned feet

a slow caress
on pedals made of wood,

his air of luminous
resolve

matched, among
your portraits, only

by the grace of one
red-shawled Miguel,

whose voice, I know,
was heard

in every mud-rich
village of the land,

and whose limbs
were later snapped

and slung
in the rising sewerage-streets of Líma,

though you glanced his
bright perfection here:

returned
from the famished ridges,

alert to what
the light unfolds,

his tilted face awash,
he grips

between his finger-tops
two trade-forbidden cocoa leaves,

and sits, hunger-firm,
but strong enough

to still, for now,
the baring instruments,

and lift
the sunken heart.

DUTCH MASTERS

An age away, the scented evergreens
are still, a lucent wave commits
to hush, the sun emits a breath,
as the noon-dim
labourings commence:
the slender, severed necks
are tossed, the throttled mouths
are mounted in the heat,
and inch by inch
the fragrant earth is stripped
of human foliage, an
evacuated island
glinting in the sun,
whose high, in-
sinuating witness, too,
is whittled down
by windy-deep sea-distances
traversed by golden ships,
the agony
drowned out,
the heady deaths annulled –
a complicated commerce
that finds its second lustre here,
in the satin cheeks
and quiffed moustache

of the *Laughing Cavalier,*
the fluorescent cuffs
and florid sash
a single flow and glimmering,
his canny, quiet eyes
a-gleam, two tiny pools
of blue and black,
pricked
by the light of the world.

THE RAID

Next to a clean, shopped shot
of Jeff Bezos's grinning head —

top, once more, of the earth's
so-called list

of fish-faced, smiling rich —
wedged below

a line in bold, that
beacons the long

longed for arrival
of this *boy who dreamed*

of colonising space,
news flaps in also

from dark-aged Sweden,
where fifteen

hundred summers past
a nameless

massacre occurred –
was schemed, that is,

and swung to gleeful,
throbbing motion –

in an island haven, walled
houses looking out

on the northern seas'
easy crash of light,

with, perhaps, the usual
fart-filled bustle

and settled ache of peace
we take for

ordinary living:
here, I learn,

some as yet unrealised
phantom gang

came slinking
with the tide

one day, and before
pickpocketing

the stock of bartered
jewels and laces, Roman coins,

along with every
shining thing, up-

turned their homely cup
of havoc

on the heads
of the island-folk,

whose now re-
surfaced bones

show signs of blunt
and subtle traumas, both:

the old man's axe-
opened skull, for instance,

dumped and singed
in the blazing hearth,

or the gentle, goof-limbed
body of a boy

who was stunned
and gnawed by sharpened clubs,

or a shapeless other, belted
clear out of time

to a mud-shattering death,
into whose

stopped mouth, after,
were shoved the teeth

of a ravenous bull.

KILLINKERE

Let them murder, scalp
and sell for gain

until the buffalo are wiped
from sight, he quipped

of the rat-
faced poachers

slinking West, adding
apothegm to adage,

that *the only good*
Indians I've ever seen

were dead —
the beloved, butch-eyed

Philip Sheridan, whose
father's people

years before
had fled

the lake-thin light
and perished earth

of Cillín Chéir, from
which infested parish air

his own turf-dull pallor
and quarried stare

no doubt derived —
the leaden prairie's

first commander,
the rising general

known elsewhere
(in private chambers

out of shot) as
a brown, rock-

brutal *little chap*,
who had his uses —

whose slooping arms
could stretch

to itch his blunted shins
while standing,

so strange and stout
an ape-like man, the still

presiding president
confided, he had

not a neck enough
to hang him.

QUESTIONING A TANK

Into the shocked, shucked shell
of the hospital at Kunduz, which

for ten days past, in streaming light
(the season's slant of sun), has spilled

a steaming trail of twisted bricks,
chewed up rails, a grieving mist – the site

where the counted, cradled sick
burned up, the still un-

bordered doctors tell, in beds
the red-blue bombers

turned to smoking tar –
into the murdered spectacle,

a spangled, metal beast, a tank,
has since arrived, to crinkle

underneath its feet
the very residues of war,

a mounting dust-heap mingled
in its wake, whose quiet particles

now drift and sway,
dissolving in the blue –

as the learned pugilographer
appears in print, enrobed

in points of lucidation, the buff
and cleanly Michael Newton,

who, pending
Pentagon investigation, will clarify

the one un-
answered question thrice

for all concerned:
Who had control, that day,

of base-defensive protocols?
Why include

a hospital
among the targets pre-approved?

And what, he wonders,
happened on the ground?

WORLD CUP

With the late-flung
weight

of his drag-tailed boot,
Akinfeev

kicked off fate
last night

and sent
a shudder trembling

through the hard, perfected
sponge of earth

and across
the watching world, Russia

shaking from its
perch on high

gigantic Spain,
bewildered

still by the un-
skilled, surging

heart of their enemy,
which won

the final field —
all this a-tingle

as word elsewhere
confirms

what stocks began
to whisper days before:

that the ripened
money mogul, Murdoch,

who squints and coughs
in the flame-blue suit

of a cartoon billionaire,
has bowed

to the might
of modern times, our age

of star-white screens
and digitised desire,

and merged
in one historic stroke

his swilling vat
of news and noise

with Disney Inc. –
Murdoch,

who clocks-in time
by phone each week

with the globe's golden-
haired commander-chief

and knows
the deal; whose

running vineyard
retreats and blooms

in splendrous colour
every year,

as the wildest Californian
fires worsen,

scorching the air
a desert red.

A STORY

In sight of the brown,
sun-graven shimmer

of Colombia's Cauca river,
on a village road,

Ibes Trujillo — who once defused
a blasting hydro-dam

out of love, he said,
of the earth and flowing water —

was kidnapped,
hacked, and bulleted

to death
(his body gone)

by machine-gun men
who flood the region weekly

like a plague, the ex-
pert monitor proclaims,

of blind extermination —
a story only told in flashes,

as the still crash-
landing cameras

pivot now
to the wet northwest,

where one teardrop-
driven CEO

has broken down
and burst the waves,

and the moon-grey,
twitching lips

of Elon Musk repeat
the recent revelation:

that to build
a human bus to Mars

and keep the massing
Model 3 on track,

this year
the Tesla head forgot

his birthday night
entirely —

no time, he
nearly wept on-air,

no break,
no nothing.

BLACK HOLE

A void

packed in
with falling light

so thick
the scaffolding collapses,

no chink of dust
or flume survives,

the cosmic tenebrum
sinks down

from black
to outer-black

forever: today
200 scientists

breathed out
as one

a folding ripple-
breath of joy,

as the first and only
images came clear

of this none-
devouring, heart-

of-shadow shape,
a monster larger

than our solar space,
roaring blankly

in the dark —
its universal upset

visioned now,
and funnel-fed

to all the Earth,
where Facebook

yesterday decreed
a lasting *tweak*

or two
to how the dead

are housed online:
from here

on in, a
sifting string

of digit-code
will pluck

their future birthdays
from the flow,

the hidden data-
mine grow still,

so remaining users'
pain is stayed,

and the tight-knit site
itself remain

a place of love
where life lives on.

STAR

The strobe-lit star
of this porn clip

grips
the leathered arm

of the nightclub chair
the sweat-

laced, shaven
gun-for-hire below her

thrusts from,
his lusive cock colossal

in the lights
that clash

from the groping lens:
she bruts her mouth

for vowels
that crack in cut-

lapse audio,
and bends to crush

her pike-eyed
partner's face

from the frame –
a lurch

that sets
the hardly sensed,

translucent hand
of the camera-man

a-shake, reeling
through the vodka-metal dark

till both appear again,
this time

in close-up
clear enough

to trace, inked
in green

at the base
of her neck: *viva,*

a word for *live,*
long live, life

itself.

ON THE LACK OF
WHAT IS FOUND THERE

From Singapore's
gleaming fountain heights,

word comes down
of James (the there-now resident)

Dyson, prim and lean
in steam-cleaned, butler-folded jeans,

who last week
found himself complete

with a water-floating
home-from-home, built

to blend mankindly ease
and cantilevered elevation

with earth itself,
above the city gardens:

that this uprooted billionaire
discerns in Britain's

broken isles
a sleek self-sovereignty of one,

a blue frontier of glory
floating out to sea —

thus setting off
a hive-like hum

across the trilling troposphere,
which over-clouds, for now,

all other noise, including
news of how

within a year or two,
through the fly-infested wastes

of Western Canada,
a funded bus will trundle,

scooping up
and putting down

the unknown reservation women
where they please,

who today, by night,
walk out as prey

to ghost-like murder-men
that cruise with pale impunity

the drifting, endless roads:
4000 dead or disappeared,

a grief-stung grandmother
remembers, *for them*

and for the future,
I hope the bus arrives.

RAZING ARDEA

Among Rome's
artful band of jester bards,

who laughed and roared
with all the learned

murderers
of curia and court,

but slept, from habit,
head to ground,

one once heard rumours
sifting through –

of ancient savageries
renewed,

and smoking fields
of oil and grain –

and sat awake, alone
for days, trans-

muting mutely
fact to myth,

until the fitful
tablets read:

When the shadow
dropped, and Turnus died,

the injured earth
went wet with blood,

and soon the sun-
white haze was dark,

as bodies vanished,
turned to char,

and soldiers
lifted flocks of fire

on streets where
Turnus once was glad —

a fog began to build
in air, of faces smeared

with tar and fear,
and everywhere

the gust of burning ash,
the deafened flesh

and guttering mouths
of children, women,

weeping men,
which as they

thinned, grew pallid,
emptied out,

took on new shape,
became one

rising silhouette:
a heron, wrought

from dying breaths,
its feathers grey

and inked with grief,
but with gold eyes

flashing, and gentle
feet, and wings to beat

the molten wind —
to keep unburied,

pulsing still, the smoking
city's ardent soul.

MY POET FRIEND

My poet friend, in love again
with broken-

fingered, sleeting life,
swings one fist

behind him as he walks,
and crocks

a gun-like camera
with the other

close to heart –
to capture crows

that flare and squat
and strut the shore

with songless urgency,
their sin-grey heads

at work on sand
like him, he says, a proof

of brute unbeauty's
lasting charms

(on this, our isle
of hidden harms).

The misting sun
dilates and breathes

in beachy light
the crows have slung

across the wind
to snag his every step;

but he believes
the poetry

of hunger and debris,
and plants his feet

in the wake of their wings –
shouting to the shadows

unspeakable things.

SLEEPER

The boy who's chasing
pigeons round the green

is bright
as all the summer:

he edges the glassy grass
at a prowl, and plans

to stun their portly strut
to flight –

he leaps! and makes them
batter the light –

his rough staccato shouts
sing out, victorious!

And all the boarded
windows blink,

as the nearby
lady, rain-dark

hair pulled
back in a bun,

slumps her shoulder
to the steel park-bench,

her two fists pressed
to the brow of her head.

WHAT STARLINGS DO

The starving starlings shoot
the noonday sun:

sporadic, flammering bursts
of flight

from wire-perch
to pavement cracks

that simmer black and grey.
Above the motley crisis

of the day, they swell
the sixteen winds of the city,

evict their secret
heart of song

with almost lexical aplomb,
pitching love-notes

with frail alarm
to the shifting, shuttered sky.

Below, street-bound,
they gutter the ground

for bits and scraps,
their scurry and hop

and bruise-blue sheen
equivocal as rain.

But when the governed air
grows large,

they blend with every
sound and sight, like

the hidden children chirping
with the crowd – about

homes for all, and human rights.

SEAPOINT

Once the curlew
slinks away

the swimmers come
back daily –

like the lady
who folds a skull-

cap brightly
round her face,

treading the bone-
grey water

in delicate bourrée;
or this other, swaying

into it, all talk,
who holds two fingers

pinched and raised,
until her head

quicks under, cold!
And here's a man

who lifts each step
with studious attention,

one arm hovering
above the rail, whose

sea-bowed eyes
reiterate the light

my late grandfather's
seemed to keep,

as he slows
his body into place,

to stand waist-deep
in the gathering tide.

THE COMMONS

Sean, our common earth's in smoke,
the shadow-rule

of feasting, famine-fed conspirators
(a sleek elite) extends

to every nook
where gladness one-time grew.

'Tis like a sunbeam
in the mist, said some other

loss-eyed wilder-man
of love, like you

a grey-sky-sodden
hierophant

of dirt in bloom
and revelry: John Clare,

whose digger's life
and empty-bellied sorrowing

you praised as *permanent*
and *true* —

in this, our age
of wilting seas

and homesick, lock-out blues.
With quick largesse,

your bursting blend
of magnanimity and vim,

in a liquor-flux of inspiration,
you reeled his verse

from memory, and pictured
peasant-crowds alit

with world-transforming rage.
I trod home across

the mossy, rain-
bewintered city's wreck

in quietness, alive
and less alone.

To feel at all: an act
of intimate dissent,

as gentle-hearted heretics
have ever felt and known.

Is this, then, our one inheritance,
the ache where voices grow?

My poem's a lifted echoing,
as if they might continue.

JOHN CLARE ENCLOSED

John Clare, your eagle's nose
grows wise and flat

on the else unsmelt
suppressions of the earth.

You knew the world particulate
and true – and here you sit,

demure in inky water-colours,
bright-berry-eyed and stately,

a water-jug at rest
in elbow-distance down the tray.

A boyish elder-look, like light,
breaks across your face; you stare

as if an age of plenty, long ago begun
in green delight and common-song,

had all dissolved, a memory,
to noise and nothingness,

some bleak *beyond*
that slips your faded, folding

fist of bones, for now —
though the groan (or grin)

that's surfacing, the watch you keep,
would make a merry mix.

My own un-peasant hunger
knows no muck or grass,

the sodden *thing like bread*
you supped for miles

that kept your famine-fingers clean,
but longs, in indolence, sweet-bitterly,

for you yourself, restored:
a five-foot shadow,

lit by wind and all at large
a-down the ringing heath —

when time, like verse,
was gentle, coarse and full.

I've heard the very sun
would touch the earthen rim, far-off,

and lead you on ... perhaps to this,
(my wisp of want, a lark's desire),

to hale the air of once, and ever,
meeting no enemy & fearing none.

BOOK OF SALT

After Catullus

Where do they go,
the storm in the sun,
the bitten skin,
the long dark
hungering
we lived within
by day, by night,
a twilit time,
the crazy moon
our witness – kissed
through risen
rooms again, again,
and again the endless
dram, replenishing...
Oh before our
numbered bones
burn out, bring
me your cup
of clearest water,
let me drink
from the poem
of your lips.

~

Rustling robes, our
hurried hands
alive in time,
the lifting flock
grew wings, a rush
flew through
the labyrinth, some charm,
or spell, unlocked
your skin – I fell
in falling waters
like a rain. An
ancient memory,
gone stale. Now
my light-smacked,
soured eyes retrace
with sudden
wisdom (envy,
too) the cunning
sun that slipped
in nets, de-
liciously down,
into the humming
cell, to find your
fingers dancing
still, a brightened
whirl – that kept

the captured sparrow
singing in its cage.

~

Generous,
        lugubrious,
abundantly aggrieved,
let the gods of love
stream down
in murmurations —
to fix the honeyed
hour, to mend
the scattered breaths!
Her feathered pet,
her gripped,
melodic joy-
machine, is
ripped of air:
a swirling dirt
reclaims the road.
Ah bird of death,
fill up the ashen
daylight, as I
murmur you
a song.

~

Hoping
my book
of petty,
languid
love-and-
life, its
polished
portraiture,
will live
beyond my
weathered
days, go on
to flood the
dry dirt road
with light, a
spilling feast,
old friend, I
gifted out
your name
last night (that
smoking furl)
to the youthful
god of hush
and fame, who
stood moon-
shadowed
at my door,

whispering
the secret word.

~

Me again, come back
to sing of tenderness
and hate. I still exist,
the callow architect,
the tough-eyed,
weeping wound,
of all this amorous
distress. You're
gone (I made
you go), so here
we are, we two,
in banishment, awash
in the bright, free-
wheeling wish
of love-for-sale
once more — unending
streams of men
like me … granted!
Alone for now,
as if forever, how
can I endure your
absence — this
broken cup

that fills my every
noon-of-night
with sunken light,
this hungry fig
now shrunk, in the
seething winter sun?

~

The latest flux
of reverential bards,
studious technicians
tinkering with words,
the laurel-loving
literate (sonorous,
assured), I daintily
re-designate: ir-
relevant, absurd.
Meticulously
mobile, mellifluous
and dull, our
generation's
metaphors are all
predictable. *Speech
is like a flower,*
so life becomes
a root, unfurling
in the suburbs

a sentimental fruit.
My volatile scatology,
revisionist, uncouth,
is bartering (in
poetry) for another
kind of truth.

~

In the dim, bare-
windowed alley-way,
where broken poets
slump and piss,
a heap of empty-
heartedness, I paused
beneath the stars,
the unheroic lover,
indelible, remiss,
and vandalised
my rancour, re-
membering your kiss.

~

Flower-face, fickle-
fingered angel
of the human race,
come cock your kingly

ears, lean in, oh grant
my lissom wish ... I long
to be your fuckboy —
slavering and rich.

~

The huge, high fury
of the wind at noon,
the blazing
desert sands (in hurled,
hard fistfuls)
blinding all the land,
the snow
that conquers light,
a dull imperium, the long,
low sun
that swells on winter days
to blue entirety,
and the plunging night
that follows, they
none of them compare
to what so gnaws
your huddled home,
cold friend — I mean
the human demon,
ravenous and lean:
Debt, the god

now tapping
at your glass.

~

A mildewed room,
high walls, a pane
of multi-seasoned,
seeping light, the
hushed, unruly bed,
upstairs, the new,
unknowing neighbours,
hot-hammering, in flight,
a muted mumble
filtering the day, the thin-
boned windiness of dawn,
a sea-breeze-freighted chill ...
all this I celebrate
and bless — before
the laughing darkness
wipes us from the map.

~

My beating
hendecasyllabus ...
it hurts.

~

I feel for
the ox-eyed daisy,
cleanly cut – or
did it wither, hurt
to death, in purest,
putrid bitterness?
The drench of love,
its wild
and supple churning,
that brought me
to the brim, my
heart, was
likewise
cut to ground
by you – disdaining
distance, muse
of all the world!
Oh let the silken roads
flow on, the sun-
deep mines
reverberate, a hail
of earthly commerce
thunder at my gate ...
I'll not be there,
the quivering voyeur,
but far away,
a spectral breeze

invisibly at work,
the emissary
of meadow-flowers,
weeping after dark.

~

The warring ships, the roar
of poisoned seas, the grim,
metallic winds go in,
with mud, with grain,
the frozen sun, the gravid,
groaning hills, and gathered
ivory of light, the brim,
the break, the flow of night,
the compacted heat
of the moon go in, with
sparrows' wings, the spew
of dying whales, the dream,
the dew, the fog of final
breaths go in, with grief
that sings in the heart,
the tears, the fallen years,
a gone-forever time,
the spite, the weight,
the touch of hands, my rain
of endless need go in,
a quiet mingling of ashes —

this urn of words
your grave.

~

All that passion,
all that hate,
kept you alive, and me —
the wounded epithet
preserved, our huge,
unending journey done,
the sky
torn up by whispers,
our skin
a midnight blue, your
steaming breath,
your gleam, your glare,
the raging heart of day
burned on
a little longer, here:
a book of salt
to kindle
the incandescent sun

THE SEA AND THE LIGHTHOUSE

Jack B. Yeats, 1947

Somewhere your life stands up
and skies arrive —
you breathe, and breath
moves through the island night,
your boots are doused
in the flow, as if
the art of motion
and the stolid rest of stones
were yours, and one.
Yesterday's hat has flown
your head
to lodge in the doff
of your flaming fist, and the wind
that grips your spilling frame
has weathers in it,
shards of lighthouse light
to fleck the baring
autumn clouds
and pierce the cloak
of the crumpled rain.
A seabird wakes
on the beating rock,
and world is here,
its flurr of heat

and lifting weight
the sound and shape
of all desire – to float with it
in the moonless air,
be filled, like
the risen pool of earth
and reeds, to the greeny rim,
with every shadow
wading
the blue salt way
you came for: there,
where lit limbs know
the tang
of held intent
and sharp arrival
(the final light
that lived inside you)
as brightness tingles
on the turning road
under the fallen
dark of a wave.

PING PONG

In the blue garden
you are playing ping pong –
blue, because

I've stumbled here,
foal-footed, head half-
lit with sleep, the grass

a prickle, a wash,
of bare blue under me,
and the air

like water, but thinned
to take my weight,
to make my scatter

through moon-big rooms
and out
to the rainless night

in which your voices float
an ease, a lightness,
light.

You are playing ping pong,
trading a volley of limb-
long yelps for breath,

the both of you re-gathered
over and over
as laughter — to dare,

to dance a new trapeze
on this, the summer's
trembling line...

and I might
be the hurried hush,
the dipping star,

the blink that brightens
at the rim,
who before his parents

turned to him, to wrap
his dream-quick
watchfulness in words,

became the bird's
heartbeat
in the singing tree,

the flown ball given
into living
memory.

INIS MEAIN

Woke early,
all the island ticking
like a maze. I walked

to lose my way
in water-lit seclusion,
found, of course, the sea —

sea through which
the reaching summer
shimmered (I saw

my feet go pink
beneath the waves).
And when

I walked again,
through the very
shunting heart of heat,

a second cuckoo
sang! And be it noted
how, from listening grass

and unbewildered rocks,
the sky-white wind
came bounding after

all the day – a sprig of birdsong
clutched in every fist.
I breathed it in. I stepped

across the beating rim.
My shadow grew longer
until the sun dipped.

BISHOP'S POOL

This poem has roots
in the sea, and time:

in Bishop's Pool, when
we slipped the plunging sun ...

and let the wrack-
blue waters

haul and hold, com-
pletely plumb

our bodies' bird-boned,
drifting shiver

down to the merrow
dark below,

where breakers
breathe

and the green foam
drops

a hundred ways
to shadow: yes,

dropped and spilled
our names afresh

as salt, and sand,
and a wind awash

with things we bring
to the sea's flame,

which now (and
every wanting season)

lay claim
to us again:

five shipwrecked
mountains, dreaming mist,

the cuckoo's eye,
the brimming nest,

the latch in the voice
and lift of pain,

the flit of a swallow
in a flense of rain,

the wave in the blood
and the swimming stone

that flows and falls
by breath alone –

like the ghosts we knew
on given nights,

soft as seals
in the soundless light.

FOUR SWANS

Not because
the days reverse,

our fingers feel
the spindrift

spinning back to rain,
or that we return

to what we were, retrieve
our dashing lives intact –

but for the motion in it,
and the catching light

it carried once,
that lives

as only dim
sensation now,

this book of wants
makes room

for the flock of swans
no battened heart

could conjure:
flung from the wreck

of Ben Wisken's bones,
they curvled heaven

round them as they shook
the airy corridors,

tagging joy
behind them like a kite –

they hit the running
breath, and ran

the island ringing
through the wave ...

and had they lit,
had they looked,

had they wheeled again,
they'd have seen

what gusting verse
can only dream:

the wind-spilled
wilderness aflow;

heard us,
the distant children,

singing down the sands.

THE CLEARING

No photograph collates
the deep climb up

those muck-blue lines
of bog-track, sloped

to set the winds awry
and bend the cloudlight

backwards into rain,
or the clambering finish after,

our bustle and whoop
and swift declension, as knees

brace down for the peaty gaps,
and voices swing for home below,

where all the afternoon
he's moved about, mowing

the rushes to a shaven green,
honing nature's art

of unpremeditation
with a cleanly disposition,

even as a blade —
memory alone retains

what need has told us life was like,
a shimmer implicated

in the faded picture falling now
through the gripping fingers of this poem,

which says in doubtful,
delving faith of time,

that somewhere still
we're paused perpetually:

on a hilltop flecked
cotton-white

and swayed to motion round us
as we rest,

our faces fixed
for larkwings on the rise,

to the high-lit spaces,
to the billowing sun,

our sky-filled breathing
holding fast.

ACKNOWLEDGEMENTS

A number of these poems have appeared in other publications: *Bread and Roses 2020* (Culture Matters), *Children of the Nation* (Culture Matters), *Elsewhere: A Journal of Place*, *Irish Marxist Review*, *Irish Pages*, *Poetry Ireland Review*, *Skylight 47*, *Smithereens Literary Magazine*, *The Galway Review*, *The North* and *The Palestine Chronicle*. Likewise, recorded versions have featured on RTÉ Radio 1's *Poetry Programme*, RTÉ Lyric FM's *Poetry File*, and Poetry Ireland's *Words Lightly Spoken* podcast. I'm grateful to the editors and organisers in each case, as well as to The Arts Council / An Chomhairle Ealaíon for the Literature Bursary I received in 2020.

This collection is dedicated to my family.